"As a pastor, I get asked lots of questions. I'm approached by unbelievers seeking to understand the gospel, new believers unsure about next steps, and maturing believers wanting help answering questions from their Christian family, friends, neighbors, or coworkers. It's in these moments that I wish I had a book to give them that was brief, answered their questions, and pointed them in the right direction for further study. Church Questions is a series that provides just that. Each booklet tackles one question in a biblical, brief, and practical manner. The series may be called Church Questions, but it could be called 'Church Answers.' I intend to pick these up by the dozens and give them away regularly. You should too."

Juan R. Sanchez, Senior Pastor, High Pointe Baptist Church, Austin, Texas

"Where can we Christians find reliable answers to our common questions about life together at church—without having to plow through long, expensive books? The Church Questions booklets meet our need with answers that are biblical, thoughtful, and practical. For pastors, this series will prove a trustworthy resource for guiding church members toward deeper wisdom and stronger unity."

Ray Ortlund, President, Renewal Ministries

Does the Old Testament Really Point to Jesus?

Church Questions

\

Does the Old Testament Really Point to Jesus?

David M. King

CROSSWAY®

WHEATON, ILLINOIS

Trade paperback ISBN: 978-1-4335-9141-9
ePub ISBN: 978-1-4335-9143-3
PDF ISBN: 978-1-4335-9142-6

Library of Congress Cataloging-in-Publication Data

Names: King, David M., 1970- author.

Title: Does the Old Testament really point to Jesus? / David M. King.

Description: Wheaton, Illinois : Crossway, 2024. | Series: Church questions | Includes index.

Identifiers: LCCN 2023019785 (print) | LCCN 2023019786 (ebook) | ISBN 9781433591419 (trade paperback) | ISBN 9781433591426 (pdf) | ISBN 9781433591433 (epub)

Subjects: LCSH: Bible. Old Testament. | Bible. New Testament—Relation to the Old Testament. | God (Christianity)

Classification: LCC BT225 .K46 2024 (print) | LCC BT225 (ebook) | DDC 221.6/1—dc23/eng/20230919

LC record available at https://lccn.loc.gov/2023019785

LC ebook record available at https://lccn.loc.gov/2023019786

Crossway is a publishing ministry of Good News Publishers.

BP		33	32	31	30	29	28	27	26	25	24
15	14	13	12	11	10	9	8	7	6	5	4	3	2	1

You search the Scriptures because you
think that in them you have eternal life;
and it is they that bear witness about me.

John 5:39

"Go get the sky hook out of the truck." That's how Eddie initiated the new guys. Eddie was a painting contractor. He hired me and a couple of my buddies as a way of tapping into a promising young labor force. High school boys need money, and my buddies and I didn't want to work at the mall. Eddie enjoyed teaching us how to paint houses and have fun at the same time.

Part of the fun was hearing him tell a rookie to go get the sky hook out of the truck.

What is a sky hook? Most guys had no clue, but they'd hurry out to the truck anyway, eager to do a good job. The rest of us would continue working, wondering how long it would take the new guy to realize that he had been sent on a painting contractor's version of a snipe hunt. Our boss's love language was practical jokes—*there is no such thing as a sky hook.*

Does the Old Testament really point to Jesus? Some Christians go looking for Christ in those first thirty-nine books of our Bibles and feel like that poor rookie rummaging through the back of the work truck, looking for something they can't find. It makes sense that the Bible would be about Jesus. But there's a nagging suspicion in the back of their minds that something isn't quite right. The Old Testament includes all sorts of stories, a whole bunch of laws, and entire books of prophecy, all of which have something to do with an ancient people called Israel. But where's Jesus? His name isn't even mentioned! Is he hiding somewhere? Is this a joke? Maybe the idea of reading the Old Testament in light of Jesus is just a spiritual version of looking for a sky hook.

Perhaps you've had thoughts like this. Maybe your pastors or disciplers keep encouraging you to read the Old Testament with a view to Christ, but you just don't see how. Of course, you don't believe that they're trying to trick you! Still, you find their understanding of Jesus in the Old Testament to be curious. When you've read the Old Testament, you haven't seen him. Either you're missing something or your well-intentioned friends are just reading into the Old Testament something that isn't there.

So which is it?

This booklet aims to help you see that the Old Testament truly is about Jesus. Specifically, I want to show you where that idea comes from, what we should (and shouldn't) understand it to mean, and why it matters for you as a Christian. No sky hooks are involved, so I hope you will follow along in good faith.

Does the Old Testament Really Point to Jesus? Jesus Thought So!

Does the Old Testament really point to Jesus? To answer that question, we should ask an expert. Who's the leading authority on Bible interpretation? It's not the dear person who first shared the gospel with you, as knowledgeable as he or she may be. It's not your pastor either, despite his wisdom and experience. It's not even a biblical scholar who has devoted an entire academic career to the study of Scripture. All these people are valuable in the formation of our faith; we should learn from them as much as we can. But the leading authority on all things spiritual—including our question about the Old Testament—is Jesus himself.

Look at Jesus's credentials. He's the beloved Son of God, the crucified and risen Savior, the Lord of heaven and earth. I assume that because you're reading this booklet, you know Jesus in this way. You've repented of your sins and believed in him for salvation; you've come to know him as the treasure of your life. If you don't know Jesus in this way, and you're just reading this booklet out of curiosity, I hope what you read here will help you understand more clearly who Jesus is and what he did—and I hope you will trust in him and be saved. As Lord of all, he's worthy of your faith.

As Lord of all, he's also the Bible expert we're looking for! Jesus is the leading authority on Bible interpretation. So if we could ask him what he thinks about the Old Testament, we would have the answer to our question.

Thankfully, if you read through the Gospels—Matthew, Mark, Luke, and John—you'll discover exactly what Jesus thought about the Old Testament. He valued it as the authoritative word of God. He studied it as a boy (Luke 2:46); he attended synagogue every week where it was read and explained (Luke 4:16); his grasp of it gained him the title Rabbi (John 1:38); he taught it with an authority that surpassed the scribes of Israel (Matt. 7:29); he insisted that it could not be broken (John 10:35); and he referred to it constantly throughout his ministry, even while struggling for breath during his crucifixion (Mark 15:34). Jesus valued God's word as authoritative.

But these observations only touch generally on Jesus's perspective on Scripture. We need to press in a bit further if we're going to find the answer to our more specific question: Did Jesus see *himself* in the Old Testament? Did he understand that the Old Testament was ultimately pointing *to him*? The answer is, He did!

The First Easter Evening

During his earthly ministry, Jesus had prepared his disciples for his resurrection from the dead—but they hadn't grasped what he meant. You can imagine their fear and wonder when he showed up among them after his crucifixion. The Gospel of Luke reports one of his appearances on that first Easter evening. Jesus had already appeared to Mary, to Peter, and to two other disciples; now he appeared to a larger group of disciples gathered in Jerusalem. After convincing them that he was truly alive, Jesus said to them,

> "These are my words that I spoke to you while I was still with you, that everything written about me in the Law of Moses and the Prophets and the Psalms must be fulfilled." Then he opened their minds to understand the Scriptures, and said to them, "Thus it is written, that the Christ should

suffer and on the third day rise from the dead, and that repentance for the forgiveness of sins should be proclaimed in his name to all nations, beginning from Jerusalem." (Luke 24:44–47)

Do you notice how Jesus helps the disciples make sense of his death and resurrection? He uses the Old Testament. He reminds them that every part of it—"the Law of Moses and the Prophets and the Psalms"—speaks of him. The Old Testament doesn't make vague, generic predictions about the Messiah either! These Scriptures, Jesus says, portray him as the Christ who dies, rises on the third day, and is proclaimed as the Savior of the world.

So, yes, Jesus saw himself in the Old Testament. According to him, the Old Testament outlines the very shape of the gospel. The name "Jesus" may not be spelled out, but the person and work of Jesus are. Jesus is the Christ, the promised ruler whose suffering, triumph, and salvation are foreshadowed all throughout the Old Testament.

The Mountainside Sermon

Earlier in his ministry, long before that first Easter, Jesus encouraged his disciples to read Scripture in light of his coming and in light of the fact that he came to fulfill God's promises. His rather startling instruction came from a sermon he preached while on a mountainside. Using "the Law or the Prophets" as a reference to the Old Testament, Jesus told the crowd,

> Do not think that I have come to abolish the Law or the Prophets; I have not come to abolish them but to fulfill them. For truly, I say to you, until heaven and earth pass away, not an iota, not a dot, will pass from the Law until all is accomplished. Therefore whoever relaxes one of the least of these commandments and teaches others to do the same will be called least in the kingdom of heaven, but whoever does them and teaches them will be called great in the kingdom of heaven. (Matt. 5:17–19)

Jesus makes it plain that the Old Testament is here to stay. He hasn't come to scrap it; nor does he intend for anyone to ignore it. So far, so good—no one on the mountainside that day would've been surprised to hear Jesus affirm Scripture in this way.

But then Jesus drops that word "fulfill." No doubt, that little word raised some eyebrows. It's a shocking claim. What kind of person says that he is going to fulfill the Old Testament? How audacious! Yet Jesus sees the Old Testament, down to the tiniest pen stroke on each letter, as uniquely focused on him. All its promises, all its prophecies, all its demands, all its judgments—he intends to take on every bit of them.

Jesus taught his disciples to read the Old Testament in a new way; not by changing the meaning of the Old Testament, but by showing them how he genuinely and truly completes the story of the Old Testament. As a result, we can't understand either the Old Testament or Jesus without looking at both. First, we come to understand Jesus in light of the Old Testament;

then, in his fulfillment of it, we come to understand the Old Testament in light of him.

The Defense Witness

One of the most profound statements Jesus makes about the Old Testament occurs during one of his conflicts with the Pharisees. Tense moments breed terse words. When being accused of blasphemy, Jesus summons multiple witnesses in his defense. John the Baptist was one witness; God the Father was another; Moses took the stand too (John 5:30–47). According to Jesus, each of these witnesses testifies on his behalf. That is, they vouch for him; *they point to him.*

Guess who else Jesus calls as a witness? The Old Testament. Don't miss what Jesus says on this occasion about the Old Testament:

> You search the Scriptures because you think that in them you have eternal life; and it is they that bear witness about me, yet you refuse to come to me that you may have life. (John 5:39–40)

The people opposing Jesus were diligent students of the Old Testament. They pored over the Scriptures as if the Scriptures themselves could give them eternal life. Yet according to Jesus, they had completely misunderstood Scripture. The Old Testament was never an end in itself, Jesus says. It was always a sign pointing to something else—to *someone* else. And Jesus is that someone! Eternal life isn't found *in* the Scriptures but *through* the Scriptures, as they bear witness to him.

In short, Jesus would have us read the Old Testament in a way that brings us to him. Otherwise we aren't reading it right.

When you look at these three episodes in Jesus's life—the first Easter evening, the mountainside sermon, and his defense of himself to the Jews—Jesus's view of the Old Testament becomes clear. He sees the gospel in it; he discerns the meaning and mission of his life from it; he understands himself to be the point of it. We may not yet fully grasp the ins and outs of what that means, but at least we have a definitive answer to our question. The Lord Jesus, the leading

authority on Bible interpretation, believes that
the Old Testament points to him. So we do well
to read the Old Testament with Jesus in view.

In fact, when we look at Jesus's authorized
spokesmen, the twelve apostles, we find that
that's exactly what they did. It's worth taking a
moment to consider what we learn from these
"Bible experts" as well.

Follow the Leader

You probably remember the children's game
follow-the-leader. Whatever the leader did,
the others were supposed to do. If the leader
jumped, the followers jumped. If the leader spun
around in circles, the followers spun around in
circles. If the leader took off running in a crazy
zigzag pattern, the followers trailed along, zig-
ging and zagging as best they could.

We don't stop following the leader when we
grow up. The game continues into adulthood,
only no longer as a game but as a (hopefully)
mature way of life. When we perceive that those
in authority are skilled and honorable, we gladly

follow their lead. We watch them, listen to them, learn from them, even imitate them.

Jesus's first disciples were no different. They carefully listened to the things Jesus taught them about the Old Testament, and they followed his lead. They learned from him how to read the Old Testament as pointing to him. Their minds had been opened to understand (Luke 24:45).

The rest of the New Testament shows just how well they understood what Jesus taught. From the way they shared the good news about Jesus to how they instructed the churches, the disciples constantly showed how promises, patterns, and prophecies in the Old Testament ultimately culminated in the person and work of Christ. Old Testament quotations and allusions fill the pages of the New Testament. The Gospels, for example, make it a point to show how Jesus fulfilled Old Testament prophecy. Acts has the apostles preaching Jesus as the promised Christ of the Old Testament. The letters use the Old Testament as a guide for doctrine and life. Revelation envisions the end of time by using rich Old Testament imagery.

Clearly the apostles didn't think of the Old Testament as an outdated relic to be set aside! When understood in light of Jesus, it's the foundation for Christian discipleship. The apostle Paul made this point plainly when he told Timothy that the "sacred writings" are able to make us "wise for salvation through faith in Christ Jesus" (2 Tim. 3:15). What sacred writings did Paul have in view? The Old Testament! In other words, Paul said that the Old Testament leads us to know, trust, and walk with Jesus. So that we don't miss it, Paul then drives home the point:

> All Scripture is breathed out by God and profitable for teaching, for reproof, for correction, and for training in righteousness, that the man of God may be complete, equipped for every good work. (2 Tim. 3:16–17)

The Old Testament is still profitable! How could it not be? Every word of it was breathed out by God himself and points to the gospel.

The Old Testament interpreted and applied in light of Jesus is necessary to the Christian life. According to Paul, our Christian maturity actually depends on it—we are incomplete and ill-equipped without the Old Testament.

Dear believer, God has given you the Old Testament so that you might know Christ and follow him better. So be sure not to minimize its relevance as you walk with Jesus. Follow the lead of the first disciples, who were following the lead of Jesus himself, in understanding that the Old Testament points to Jesus.

How Does the Old Testament Point to Jesus?

It's not hard to see that Jesus and the apostles understood the Old Testament as ultimately pointing to Christ. The difficulty comes when you open the Old Testament to see Jesus, and he's seemingly nowhere to be found. What are you to do? Maybe if you stare at it for a while without blinking he will magically appear! Or maybe you could do some free association: "This passage of Scripture reminds me of Jesus in this way . . ."

Thankfully we don't need to resort to magic tricks or imaginative interpretation or allegory to see Christ in the Old Testament. The Old Testament *genuinely* points to Jesus—we just need to learn how.

A starter kit would be helpful. On Amazon you can get a starter kit for virtually anything: growing bonsai trees, building a carburetor, beekeeping, even tattooing. Well, Amazon doesn't sell a starter kit for seeing Christ in the Old Testament, but the Bible itself is the perfect starter kit. If we take the cues given to us in the Old Testament, coupled with examples of interpretation found in the New Testament, we begin to see how it all points to Jesus.

The Old Testament points to Jesus in six basic ways: *promises*, *shadows*, *instructions*, *fallenness*, *story*, and *themes*. Let's take a look at each in turn.

Promises

One of the chief ways the Old Testament points to Jesus is through promises God made to send a Savior into the world. These divine promises are found throughout the Old Testament. Sometimes people refer to them as *messianic promises* or *messianic prophecies*. That's a good description since *Messiah* is the Hebrew title for God's promised Savior. *Christ* is the Greek title meaning the same thing, which explains why the apostles were eager to help people identify Jesus as the Christ. The messianic hope of the Old Testament is fulfilled in him.

You won't get past the opening chapters of the Bible without encountering the first promise of a Savior. God speaks directly to the serpent, who had successfully tempted Adam and Eve to sin:

> I will put enmity between you and the
> woman,
> and between your offspring and her
> offspring;
> he shall bruise your head,
> and you shall bruise his heel.
> (Gen. 3:15)

The paint hasn't even dried on the first sin in human history when God graciously promises to send a Savior. From this point forward, we begin looking for one born of a woman ("her offspring"), who will suffer when dealing with evil ("you shall bruise his heel") and through his suffering will triumph ("he shall bruise your head"). We don't know his name yet, but already we are seeing Jesus.

As the Old Testament unfolds, God's promise to send a Savior becomes more defined. We learn that the offspring of the woman will be a descendent of Abraham (Gen. 17:7–8), from the tribe of Judah (Gen. 49:10), and in the line of David (2 Sam. 7:12–13). He will be a Moses-like prophet (Deut. 18:15) and rule as an eternal priest-king (Ps. 110:2–4). He will suffer (Isa. 53:3–11), rise from the dead (Ps. 16:10), and be enthroned as Savior of the world (Dan. 7:13–14).

We've only scratched the surface. It's been estimated that the Old Testament contains over four hundred prophetic promises dealing with a coming Savior. Regardless of the exact number, whenever you read one of these promises, lift up your eyes to the horizon. Look for Jesus, because in him all God's saving promises find their Yes and Amen (2 Cor. 1:20).

Shadows

Another way the Old Testament points to Jesus is through shadows. Isn't that a strange thing to say? What exactly is a shadow in Scripture?

You've seen your shadow before. Your shadow doesn't give you a sharp picture of who you are. If the sun were positioned just right, someone might be able to guess your height or weight by looking at your shadow. But they wouldn't be able to discern your skin color, read your facial expression, or see what clothes you are wearing—that's not how shadows work. Shadows are less about precision and more about suggestion. They show you the general shape of a thing.

God has placed shadows of Jesus in the Old Testament. In these shadows, God means for us to see the general shape of who Jesus is and what Jesus will do. We see shadows of Jesus in people like Adam, whom the Bible calls a "type" of Christ (Rom. 5:14). Adam was made in God's image, was the head of humanity, and was charged with ruling the earth for the glory of God. Yet Adam fell, plunging the world into death. Then came Jesus, the true and better Adam! Jesus succeeds where Adam failed. He creates a new humanity, bringing life out of death for all who are joined to him in faith. Even now he rules from heaven, spreading God's glory throughout the earth. If you want to learn more about how Adam was a shadow of Jesus, read Romans 5:12–21.

The Old Testament temple was also a shadow of Jesus. The temple was the dwelling place of God. It's where God welcomed his people through sacrifice, teaching his people in ceremonies what the Savior would accomplish in person. Through his death and resurrection, Jesus would fulfill all that the temple foreshadowed (John 2:19–21). No longer do we meet with God in the holiest of places; now we meet with him in the holiest of persons—in his Son,

Jesus Christ, in whom "all the fullness of God was pleased to dwell" (Col. 1:19).

There are many shadows of Jesus in the Old Testament. As you learn to read Scripture like Jesus and the apostles, you will see them everywhere. God means for us to see the general shape of Jesus's life and ministry in the sacrifices (Heb. 10:1–10); circumcision (Col. 2:11); the dietary laws and holy days (Col. 2:16); Melchizedek (Heb. 7:1–3); Moses (Acts 3:22); David (the Psalms; Matt. 1:1); Solomon (Luke 11:31); Jonah (Matt. 12:40–41); Israel (Matt. 2:14–15); the priesthood (Heb. 7:1–25); and more.

The apostle Paul summarizes it in a way we can easily remember:

> These are a shadow of the things to come, but the substance belongs to Christ. (Col. 2:17)

Not everything in the Old Testament is a shadow of Jesus. Which means you don't want to see shadows where there are none, but you definitely don't want to miss the ones that are there because the substance of those shadows is Jesus himself.

You might be wondering, *How can I tell what's a shadow and what isn't?* Well, the easiest way to identify shadows in the Bible is by reading the Old Testament in light of the New Testament. As the previous paragraphs show, the New Testament provides plenty of commentary on what elements of the Old Testament foreshadow Jesus. How do we know that Old Testament sacrifices point to Jesus? Because John the Baptist calls Christ "the Lamb of God, who takes away the sin of the world" (John 1:29). How do we know that the tabernacle points to Christ? Because the apostle John tells us that Christ "tabernacled" among us (John 1:14, author's translation). How do we know Jonah's three days in the belly of the great fish foreshadow Jesus's three days in the grave? Jesus says that it does (Matt. 12:39). The more you pay attention to how Jesus and the apostles read the New Testament, the more you'll see how the Old Testament is filled with patterns that anticipate the coming of Christ.

Instruction

Instruction is another way the Old Testament points to Jesus. This pointer is so obvious that it's easy to overlook, like something hiding in plain sight. Yet we are meant to see Jesus in Old Testament instructions.

By *instruction*, I don't mean just any instruction you happen to run across. For example, when Jacob tells his sons to go buy grain in Egypt (Gen. 42:2) or when David commands every man to strap on his sword (1 Sam. 25:13), we aren't learning something about Jesus. Rather, the kind of instruction that points to Jesus is instruction intended for God's people as a whole.

In the Old Testament, we find instruction for God's people mainly in the law code and in the wisdom writings (e.g., Exodus, Leviticus, Numbers, Deuteronomy, Job, Psalms, Proverbs, Ecclesiastes).

In the law and in wisdom, God is teaching his people how to live. Israel was under covenant obligation to follow God's instruction.

What does that have to do with Jesus? Everything! Jesus kept all those laws. Jesus embodied all that wisdom. Jesus is *the* law keeper (Matt. 5:17); Jesus is *the* wise man (1 Cor. 1:30). All the instruction God gave Israel was fulfilled in Jesus.

Have you ever thought about Jesus reading the Bible? Imagine him leaning over the desk in the synagogue, studying the sacred scrolls. I bet he never got bogged down in Leviticus! Here's the thing: When Jesus read Leviticus (or any other part of the law), he saw himself. That is, Jesus saw what God required of him as a true Israelite and faithful Son—and he obeyed. The same was true when Jesus read from the wisdom writings, like Proverbs. He understood that Proverbs was for him—that he must walk in wisdom by fearing the Lord in all the ways Proverbs describes.

What an exciting realization! As you read God's instruction in law and wisdom, you're reading what Jesus read and, more importantly, you're reading what Jesus believed and obeyed. These are the Scriptures that filled his mind and heart. These are the Scriptures that undergirded his view of sin and righteousness. These are the Scriptures that informed his practical decisions. These are the Scriptures that served as the background to everything he taught.

So don't overlook how instruction points to Jesus. Whenever you read God's instruction to Israel, you're seeing the very shape of Jesus's life.

Fallenness

As you become familiar with the Old Testament, one thing you'll notice is just how much time is spent focusing on sin. Everything moves along swimmingly for two whole chapters (Gen. 1–2)—until Adam shakes his fist at God. From that moment on, human history becomes littered with disobedience, suffering, and death.

Virtually every page of the Old Testament testifies to our fallenness. Adam the law breaker was just the beginning. Following on his heels is Cain the brother killer, Noah the alcohol abuser, Ham the father mocker, and the whole earth as Babel builders. After the call of

Abraham, things don't improve. From there on we see jealousy, deceit, incest, grumbling, sickness, disease, barrenness, drought, famine, prostitution, adultery, homosexuality, and all manner of covenant unfaithfulness. Jesus didn't mince words when he said, referring to the entire Old Testament, that there was blood from Abel to Zechariah (Luke 11:51).

How does our fallenness point to Jesus? It shows our need for him! Israel needed a Savior; the nations needed a Savior; we need a Savior. So we praise God that "Christ Jesus came into the world to save sinners" (1 Tim. 1:15). Jesus took our fallenness on himself, atoning for our sin and triumphing over evil. His death and resurrection signal the beginning of new life and the coming of a new world.

In short, Jesus is the solution to our fallenness. Picture every Old Testament instance of sin and suffering rising up and crying out for a Savior, and you'll see Jesus everywhere. All the fallenness of the Old Testament points to him.

Story

The Old Testament is filled with exciting stories. What are your favorites? I love the Joseph narrative in Genesis, the Red Sea crossing in Exodus; the fall of Jericho in Joshua, the soap opera of Samson in Judges, all the stories of Saul and David in 1–2 Samuel, and, of course, the fiery furnace and lions' den in Daniel. There are tons of great stories in the Old Testament.

But we need to realize that these stories don't stand alone in isolation from each other. Rather, they're all connected to one, sweeping, grand story. As you grasp the big story of the Old Testament, you begin to see how the little stories point to Jesus.

What is the big story of the Old Testament? It's the story of God's promised kingdom. That story unfolds through God's covenants (his relational commitments) to Adam, Noah, Abraham, Israel, and David. Together these covenants form the overall plot of the Old Testament.[1] Following Adam's failure, God promises to send a ruler to save the world; the covenant with Noah ensures there will be a world to save; and the covenants with Abraham, Israel, and David reveal through whom the ruler will come and what his rule will look like.

The Old Testament story ends without God's kingdom promises coming to pass. It's a cliffhanger, leaving us hoping for a future day when all will be fulfilled. Spoiler alert: fulfillment comes in Jesus! When Jesus arrives, establishing a new covenant, the dawn of God's kingdom has begun. Jesus is the climax of the big story, the resolution to the plot, the long-awaited King.

All the little stories fit into the big story of the promised kingdom. They all point to the surprising ways that God saves his people through a redeemer, even as circumstances threaten to derail God's promises. How will God fulfill his promise to send a ruler when Abraham's wife is barren? When Jacob is a deceiver? When famine threatens to wipe out the chosen family? When Israel is enslaved in Egypt? When giants occupy the promised land? When judges are dishonorable and kings are disobedient? When God's people ignore God's prophets? When Haman plots the genocide of the Jews? When Jerusalem sits in ruins? In all these accounts, God's surprising acts of deliverance repeat the plot of the Bible's much larger story: God, by his own sheer grace, loves to seek and save the lost.

We need to see that the little stories of the Old Testament are the backstory to the big story—that they're all part of *the story*—that story is about Jesus.

Themes

One last way the Old Testament points to Jesus is through themes. In the Old Testament, we're introduced to themes such as holiness, sin, righteousness, faith, justice, judgment, wrath, mercy, love, holiness, curse, blessing, pride, humility, election, and substitution (to name a few). All these themes prepare us for Jesus. Through them, God is like a gardener getting the soil of our minds ready for the gospel to grow. We need only to consider how each theme relates to the gospel, and we will understand Jesus better.

Take forgiveness as just one example. God forgiving sinners is a prominent theme in the Old Testament. Consider this stunning truth about God:

> He does not deal with us according to
>   our sins,
>   nor repay us according to our
>   iniquities.
> For as high as the heavens are above the
>   earth,
>   so great is his steadfast love toward
>   those who fear him;
> as far as the east is from the west,
>   so far does he remove our
>   transgressions from us.
>   (Ps. 103:10–12)

This stunning truth raises serious questions. Is God unconcerned about justice? Are our transgressions no big deal? Is he sweeping our sins under the rug? No way! If we trace this theme through the Bible, we find ourselves at a bloody cross. Only when we think about forgiveness in light of the gospel do we begin to see Jesus more clearly. God's forgiveness may be free, but it wasn't cheap. Our debt was paid by Jesus.

Other themes similarly point to Jesus. In the story of Abraham, we begin to learn about justification by faith; in the laws about sacrifice, we begin to learn about substitutionary atonement; in the prophecy of Daniel, we begin to learn about the final judgment and the resurrection of the dead. On and on the examples go. Whatever theme you encounter in the Old Testament, take it to Jesus. That's why God put it there.

Why Does It Matter Whether the Old Testament Points to Jesus?

As I write these words, a young mother in my church is preparing to go to the doctor. For years her health has declined with no diagnosis. But yesterday, following an MRI of her brain, the doctor called a meeting. The MRI has revealed a problem, maybe *the* problem.

You can imagine the strange mixture of anxiety and eagerness she feels—eagerness to receive an answer to her mysterious condition and anxiety about what the answer might be. So much depends on the doctor reading that MRI report correctly.

Is it a big deal whether the Old Testament points to Jesus? As long as you read your Bible, that's the main thing, right? I hope you're beginning to realize that a lot more is at stake. Like a doctor giving an accurate diagnosis, so much depends on us not just reading the Bible but reading it *the right way*.

Here are several reasons why it matters that the Old Testament points to Jesus.

Because Jesus Is Truthful

I don't mean for this reason to sound snarky, but it's worth repeating what we saw at the beginning of this book: Jesus said that all Scripture points to him—and Jesus isn't a liar. Nor is he mistaken. If in fact the Old Testament does not point to him, then he was either wrong or deceptive. Either of those possibilities is unthinkable! If Jesus was confused about the Old Testament, what else might have been muddled in his mind? Worse, if he was lying about it, what kind of person is he? If you can't trust what Jesus says about the Old Testament, you can't trust him at all.

But Jesus is truthful. Like his Father, all is light in him with no darkness at all (1 John 1:5). Which means you can trust him in everything— from saving you to teaching you to read the Old Testament the right way.

Because the Whole Bible Is Valuable

Have you ever seen those little pocket Bibles? To make them compact enough to fit in your pocket, publishers will leave out most of the Old Testament. Sadly what is gained in size is lost in value. To be sure, a partial Bible is better than no Bible! But a whole Bible is best.

Jesus once said (quoting from a book of the Bible you won't find in a pocket edition), "Man shall not live by bread alone, but by every word that comes from the mouth of God" (Matt. 4:4, quoting Deut. 8:3). We live by every word God has spoken, including all the Old Testament words. Not one of those Old Testament words has fallen to the ground; each one remains relevant to your discipleship. If read the right way, they "are able to make you wise for salvation through faith in Christ Jesus" (2 Tim. 3:15).

That's because the Old Testament is God's word about God's Son. It's Christian Scripture that brings you to Jesus, teaching you to trust and treasure him, to be transformed in him, and to tell the nations about him. The whole Bible is valuable for your life in Christ.

Because Error Is Dangerous

If we fail to appreciate how the Old Testament points to Jesus, then we end up in error. If we're not reading the Old Testament in light of the gospel, we'll tend to read the stories merely as behavioral object lessons, to overlook the shadows, to mine the law and wisdom for handy life principles, and to let important themes run off into the woods rather than keeping them on a gospel path.

The results are dangerous. The Old Testament is reduced to a Christless moral code, a magic book with incantations for health and wealth, or a policy manual for civic religion. Worst of all, when Jesus is absent from our interpretation, we begin relating to God apart from the only one who can bring us to God—and that's futile! For there is "one mediator between God and men, the man Christ Jesus" (1 Tim. 2:5). The truth is, there is no Old Testament example you can follow, no command you can obey, no warning you can heed, no repentance you can offer, no worship you can give to God apart from Jesus.

The error may be dangerous, but the solution is simple: Keep your eyes on Jesus as you read the Old Testament! Ask yourself how the passage points to him; ask yourself how his life, death, and resurrection reflect back on the passage. Then you will see more clearly both the truth of the passage and how it applies to your life.

Because Church Health Is Important

Of course, you want to be part of a healthy church. But what makes a church healthy? Of all the helpful answers that might be given, the most important answer is Jesus—not Background Jesus or Marginal Jesus or Unbiblical Jesus but Jesus as revealed in Scripture, standing in the middle of everything. Center Stage Jesus! Show me a church where the Lord Jesus Christ is the focus of preaching and fellowship—where the gospel is announced, acclaimed, and applied from every part of the Bible, and where people are seeking to love and live for the kingdom of Christ—and I'll show you a healthy church. At the very least, I'll show you a church growing in health. It cannot be otherwise. When the head of the church is honored, the body will thrive (Eph. 1:22–23).

Some churches place other things besides Jesus on center stage, like inspirational worship, exciting events, a beautiful campus, or social ministry. But anything other than Jesus on center stage undermines church health. The priority of the apostles should be the practice of every local church:

> Him we proclaim, warning everyone and teaching everyone with all wisdom, that we may present everyone mature in Christ. (Col. 1:28)

Christ is both the means and the end of our maturity. In him alone do we become the people God destined us to be. So find a church that doesn't ignore Christ in the Old Testament or ignore the Old Testament altogether. A church that keeps its spotlight trained on Jesus as seen in all of Scripture will likely be a healthy church.

Because We Need the Whole Jesus

When my daughter was young, she jokingly drew a picture of James from the Bible. James had no head or chest or arms, only legs and feet. I had told her that the book of James was likely written by the half brother of Jesus, and she had drawn the half brother! Let that funny drawing serve as a parable for why the Old Testament is so important. If all you know is the New Testament, you're seeing only a half Jesus. It's through the whole Bible that you come to know the whole Jesus. So don't ignore, minimize, or reject the Old Testament as you follow Christ. Rather, love the Old Testament as God's word that points you to Jesus in all his glorious fullness.

Recommended Resources

Iain M. Duguid, *Is Jesus in the Old Testament?*, Basics of the Faith (Phillipsburg, NJ: P&R, 2013).

Nick Roark and Robert Cline, *Biblical Theology: How the Church Faithfully Teaches the Gospel* (Wheaton, IL: Crossway, 2018).

Trent Hunter and Stephen Wellum, *Christ from Beginning to End: How the Full Story of Scripture Reveals the Full Story of Christ* (Grand Rapids, MI: Zondervan, 2018).

David Murray, *Jesus on Every Page: 10 Simple Ways to Seek and Find Christ in the Old Testament* (Nashville: Thomas Nelson, 2013).

Notes

1. For more on this idea see Peter J. Gentry and Stephen J. Wellum, *God's Kingdom through God's Covenants: A Concise Biblical Theology* (Wheaton, IL: Crossway, 2015).

Scripture Index

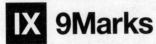

IX 9Marks

Building Healthy Churches

9Marks exists to equip church leaders with a biblical vision and practical resources for displaying God's glory to the nations through healthy churches.

To that end, we want to see churches characterized by these nine marks of health:

1. Expositional Preaching
2. Gospel Doctrine
3. A Biblical Understanding of Conversion and Evangelism
4. Biblical Church Membership
5. Biblical Church Discipline
6. A Biblical Concern for Discipleship and Growth
7. Biblical Church Leadership
8. A Biblical Understanding of the Practice of Prayer
9. A Biblical Understanding and Practice of Missions

Find all our Crossway titles and other resources at 9Marks.org.

John Onwuchekwa · Church Questions

Sam Emadi · Church Questions

Mark Dever · Church Questions

Do I Feel Like Going to Church?
Church Questions

What Is a Church?
Matthew Emadi · Church Questions

How Do I Get Started in Evangelism?
Mack Stiles · Church Questions

How Can Women Thrive in the Local Church?
Keri Folmar · Church Questions

Baptized?
Church Questions

Who's in Charge of the Church?
Sam Emadi · Church Questions

How Can I Serve My Church?
Matthew Emadi · Church Questions

How Can I Love Church Members with Different...?
Jonathan & Andy Naselli · Church Questions

IX 9Marks Church Questions

Providing ordinary Christians with sound and
accessible biblical teaching by answering
common questions about church life.

For more information, visit crossway.org.